Cockroach

Karen Hartley,
Chris Macro
and Philip Taylor

Heinemann
LIBRARY

First published in Great Britain by Heinemann Library
Halley Court, Jordan Hill, Oxford OX2 8EJ
a division of Reed Educational and Professional Publishing Ltd.
Heinemann is a registered trademark of Reed Educational & Professional Publishing Limited.

OXFORD MELBOURNE AUCKLAND
JOHANNESBURG BLANTYRE GABORONE
IBADAN PORTSMOUTH NH CHICAGO

Designed by Celia Floyd
Illustrations by Alan Fraser [Pennant Illustration]
Printed and bound in Hong Kong/China by South China Printing Co. Ltd.

03 02 01 00 99
10 9 8 7 6 5 4 3 2 1

ISBN 0 431 01685 2

British Library Cataloguing in Publication Data

Hartley, Karen
  Cockroach. - (Bug books)
  1.Cockroaches- Juvenile literature
  I.Title II.Macro, Chris
  595.7'28

Acknowledgements
The Publishers would like to thank the following for permission to reproduce photographs:
Ardea: P Goetgheluck pp6, 10, 22, E Lindgren p11, J Mason pp14, 24, 27, A Weaving pp12, 26; Bruce Coleman Ltd: A Purcell p19, K Taylor pp13, 21, 23, 25, 28, C Varndell p16, R Williams p5; Trevor Clifford: p29; NHPA: ANT p9, G Bernard p17, S Dalton p4, M Garwood p18, D Heuclin p20; Okapia: M Kage p7, N Lange p8; Oxford Scientific Films: D Curl p15.

Cover photographs: Gareth Boden (child); S Dalton, NHPA (cockroach).

Every effort has been made to contact copyright holders of any material reproduced in this book. Any omissions will be rectified in subsequent printings if notice is given to the Publisher.

Any words appearing in the text in bold, **like this**, are explained in the Glossary.

Contents

What are cockroaches?

Cockroaches are **insects** that live in lots of different countries. They are **pests** because they carry harmful **germs** which can make people ill.

There were cockroaches in the world about 300 million years ago when some of the dinosaurs were living. Today there are over 3500 different kinds of cockroach.

What do cockroaches look like?

Cockroaches have quite flat bodies with three main parts. They have six long, slim legs. Some people say that they look as though their bodies have been made out of **tortoiseshell**.

Cockroaches have two pairs of wings. They have a pair of long **feelers** on their heads. They have long hairy legs and small claws on their feet.

How big are cockroaches?

Some cockroaches are big and some are small. In Europe the cockroaches are quite small and some of them can fit on a small button or coin.

Cockroaches that live in hot countries can be much bigger. They can be as much as 9 cm long – as long as an **adult's** middle finger.

How are cockroaches born?

Some **females** lay their eggs in cases, sometimes called purses. The purses are important because they protect the eggs and stop them from drying out.

Some cockroaches will carry their eggs until they are ready to **hatch**. This might take eight weeks. When the babies hatch out of the eggs they do not have wings.

How do cockroaches grow?

Young cockroaches are called **nymphs**. As they get bigger their skin cannot stretch, so they grow a new skin and **moult** the old one.

Some cockroaches moult and lose their old skin about once a week. They do this six or eight times before they are fully grown.

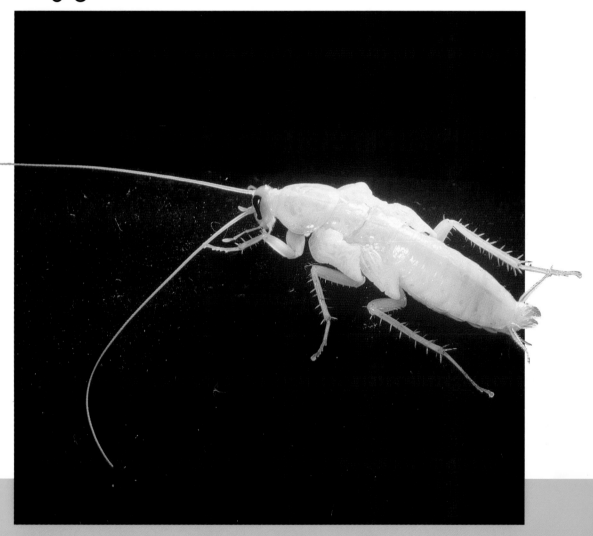

What do cockroaches eat?

Cockroaches eat dead plants or animals, like this centipede, but they will eat almost anything. They will even eat the glue from the back of postage stamps.

Some kinds of cockroaches live in hot countries like Barbados. They eat lots of different things there. They especially like the wood from dead trees.

Which animals attack cockroaches?

Lizards, frogs and birds like to eat cockroaches if they can catch them. In places like India and South America some people will catch cockroaches and eat them.

Other **insects** sometimes eat cockroaches. Some cockroaches can roll into a ball and tuck in their legs to protect themselves.

Where do cockroaches live?

Most cockroaches like to live in warm places and cannot **survive** in cold places. In Europe many live in warm buildings, but there are some kinds that live outdoors in the grass and in bushes.

Cockroaches are **scavengers**. They live in bakeries, kitchens and restaurants where they can look for scraps of food. Most choose to live indoors so they find more food.

How do cockroaches move?

Cockroaches have long legs and can run very fast. They usually move with their heads down because they are interested in looking on the ground for food.

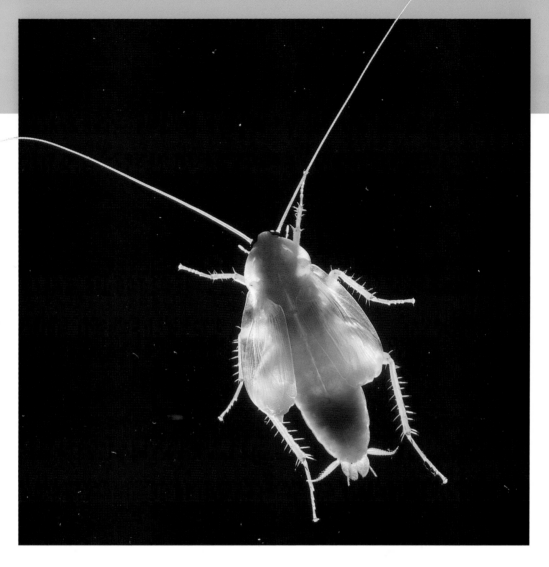

Even though they have two pairs of
wings only some cockroaches can fly.
The **females** have smaller wings and
very few of them can fly.

Some cockroaches live for a few months. Others can live for two or three years and can take one and a half years to become a fully grown **adult**.

The temperature makes a difference to how long the adult cockroaches will live. They live longer when the weather is cool but not when it is too cold.

What do cockroaches do?

Most cockroaches are **nocturnal** so they come out to look for food at night. If they see a bright light some kinds of cockroach will run away from it.

Cockroaches are called **pests** because they crawl over our food and leave dirt and **germs** on it. If we ate the food it would probably make us ill.

How are cockroaches special?

Cockroaches are very important to both plants and animals because they make the soil better. They break up dead leaves and animal droppings.

Cockroaches have two special little **feelers** at the back end of their bodies. These can feel the air being moved when other animals are close. This tells the cockroaches when they are in danger.

Thinking about cockroaches

This mother cockroach is carrying a special purse. Can you remember why she carries the purse with her?

We move air to keep us cool when it is hot. What does moving air tell the cockroach about other animals?

Bug map

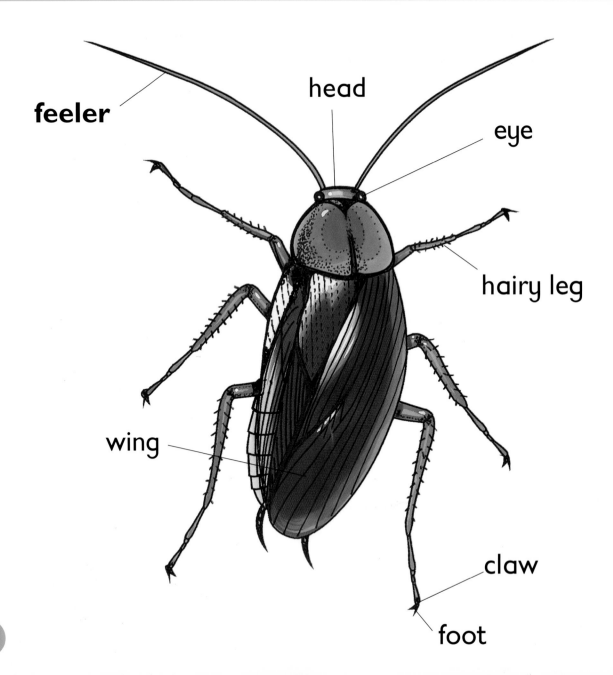

feeler

head

eye

hairy leg

wing

claw

foot

Glossary

adult a grown-up

feelers thin growths from the head of an insect that help the insect to know what is around it

female a girl

germs tiny creatures that cause diseases

hatch when an animal comes out of its egg

insect a small animal with six legs

moult when a baby animal grows too big for its skin, it grows a new one and wriggles out of the old one

nocturnal an animal that sleeps in the day and comes out at night

nymph a baby cockroach

pests animals which are a nuisance to people

scavengers animals which eat dead plants and other dead animals. Cockroaches also eat leftover scraps of food.

survive able to live

tortoiseshell something which looks very shiny like the shell on a tortoise

Index